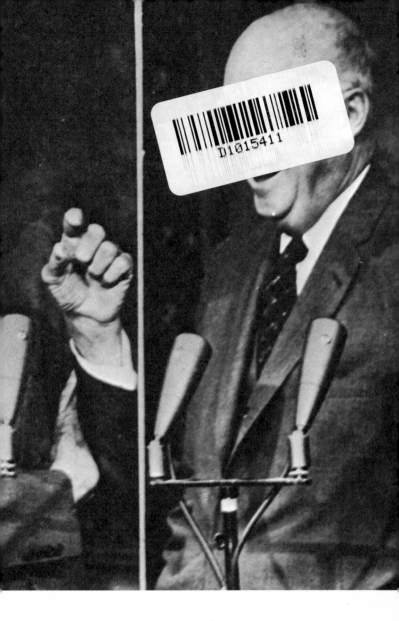

Ike strikes a variety of moods during a press conference in 1959.

IKE

To
Aunt Mary Ellen

From
Diane and John

IKE

A Great American

With an

Introduction by

Mamie Doud Eisenhower

Selected by Don Ramsey

Hallmark Editions

My Memories of Ike

BY MAMIE DOUD EISENHOWER

The inspirational qualities of Dwight Eisenhower—his buoyant disposition, his enthusiasm for life, his courage and determination—have been mentioned over and over by those who knew him. People who visited with him even briefly came away feeling better, their spirits uplifted. This was true even during the long months of his final illness.

Occasionally, someone asks me if these same characteristics carried through into Ike's private life. I can answer that best by saying that when Ike came home—whether "home" was the White House, our Gettysburg place, or, in our earlier years, a couple of cramped rooms at some

3

Army post—the house came alive. When he left on a trip or even for the day's work, the house sagged.

This is not to say that our life was all moonlight and roses. We had our disappointments and our troubles, some of them devastating, and, like any other couple, we had occasional disagreements. Yet between us there was a deep understanding, a feeling of contentment in each other's company. Sometimes, during our last years together at Gettysburg, we would sit for a whole evening on our enclosed porch, Ike busy at his painting and I reading or playing solitaire. Even in this companionable silence, I felt his inner strength and was happy in his presence.

Ike's ability to inspire others was no public facade. It was part of his being. I think it came from his abiding faith in humanity, his dedication to the simple old virtues and above all from his unfailing belief in and love for his country.

I learned very early in our married life about his single-minded devotion to America. Our first home was a suite of two small rooms at Fort Sam Houston in San Antonio. For lack of space, Ike kept his bedroll and other traveling accouterments behind a piano in one corner of the tiny living room. One day about a month after we were married, he came home early in

Ike and Mamie standing on the steps of San Antonio's Saint Louis College in 1916. Lt. Eisenhower coached football there.

the afternoon and silently proceeded to get his bedroll and other items. With sinking heart, I realized what this meant. On the verge of tears, I said: "You're not going to leave me this soon after our wedding day, are you?" Ike put his arm around me and said gently: "Mamie, there's one thing you must understand. My country comes first and always will; you come second."

It was quite a shocker for a 19-year-old bride, and for a little while after he left I cried and felt sorry for myself. Later I came to be enormously proud of a husband who felt this way about duty and country....

Ike and I first met at Fort Sam Houston one Sunday afternoon in 1915, when my parents and I stopped off at the fort to say hello to a friend, Mrs. Hunter Harris, wife of a major. As we were chatting with her, she spotted Ike across the street and called to him to come over and "meet some friends." He called back that he was on guard duty and about to start an inspection trip. "He's the woman-hater of the post," Mrs. Harris confided to me. But she did prevail on him to cross the street and be introduced.

He looked me over carefully and, to the surprise of everyone, invited me to go with him on his inspection rounds. Now I have always hated walking any great distance, but that "woman-hater" business was a red flag to me. Besides, he was just about the handsomest male I had ever seen. I accepted, and as we started around he said to me stiffly: "Now, Miss Doud, this is an Army post, and the men in the barracks are not expecting ladies. I suggest that you keep your eyes to the front."

Of course I immediately looked both to the left and the right—to his obvious discomfiture. Yet, I think he was intrigued. Long years later, telling of our first meeting in his book *At Ease,* he said with relish that I had a "saucy" face and attitude.

In any event, he began calling on me regularly at our winter home in San Antonio. I had a few other beaux, and I wasn't about to give them up immediately. But Ike was never easily discouraged. He simply out-persisted the competition, and in a few months we became engaged.

We had decided to postpone our marriage until after my 20th birthday, in November 1916, but by the spring of that year war clouds were gathering. Toward the end of June, he phoned me in Denver and said: "Let's get married *now.*"

My parents were away on a trip, and by the time they returned Ike was already on his way to Denver. They raised the roof—they had the old-fashioned notion that quick weddings weren't quite decent. But I was stubborn. Finally, Mama gave in and pretty soon she brought Papa around. We were married on July 1, 1916.

Incidentally, Mama was always very much pro-Ike. After we were married, I learned quickly not to run to her seeking comfort when my husband and I had a spat. She always sided with Ike. The two had a great liking and respect for each other, and over the years they developed a wonderful relationship.

When we arrived back in San Antonio after our wedding, I had a great deal to learn about being a wife. I had led a sheltered life and doubtless was a bit spoiled. I probably needed a little Army-type discipline, and Ike applied it, gently but firmly, when he felt it was necessary.

I had a little money left over from a cash wedding present which my parents had given us, and I hoarded it like a miser. One day during our first months of marriage, I got angry at Ike about some trivial matter. We were sitting at our little makeshift dining table, and to emphasize my point and my anger, I slapped my hand down hard on the back of his hand, which was resting on the table. My ring struck the amethyst in his West Point ring and split it wide

8

This portrait of Mamie was taken in July, 1916--the month she married Ike.

open. He looked at it sadly for a moment, then said very quietly: "Young lady, for that fit of temper, you will buy me a new amethyst with your own money." And I did—although parting with those dollars almost killed me.

Over the years we lived at many Army posts. Sometimes our quarters were pretty terrible. In Panama we lived on the edge of the jungle, and the wild animals screamed all night. Our house was inhabited by enormous tropical bugs of many kinds, by bats and even by bedbugs until I eliminated them. Our quarters at Gettysburg during World War I—Ike was training troops at an encampment near there—were so poorly heated that I thought I was going to freeze to death.

There were hard times in other ways, too. The hardest of all were the long periods when we were separated because there was no place for a wife where Ike was stationed. When our first son, Doud Dwight, whom we always called "Icky," was born, Ike was far away, and it was three days before he knew he had a son. He came to idolize that youngster, and when Icky died of scarlet fever in early childhood, for a long time it was as if a shining light had gone out in Ike's life. Throughout all the years that followed, the memory of those bleak days was a deep inner pain that never seemed to diminish much.

I think I learned to be a good wife. As Ike rose in rank and his responsibilities grew, I tried very hard to make our home a place of calmness and good cheer, where he could relax in the midst of his strenuous life. He was not the sort of husband who brought his big problems home for discussion and advice, and I rarely intruded in such matters. I knew he already had the best counsel he could get from brilliant advisers and that in due course he would make his own decision. He didn't need *that kind* of help from me.

I do know that at times he went through a great deal of inner turmoil when some momentous decision was pending. Yet he was not a worrier. Sometimes, after a day when he had to make some fateful decision, I have heard him say almost inaudibly as he lay in bed: "God, I did the best I could today." Then he would turn over and go to sleep. He was a man of great inner strength.

There was one occasion when Ike asked me to help him make a very big decision. It was early in 1956, and despite his serious heart attack the previous year, there was great pressure on him to run again. He consulted his advisers, his doctors, a number of close friends, his brother Milton, our son John—and me. Milton and John opposed a second term because they felt he wasn't up to it physically. I knew, however, that he desired nothing so much as to continue the policies and work he had begun his first term; I feared that for him to quit in the middle of things, to abandon what he deeply believed was his duty to his country, would do more violence to his health than to serve another four years. So I told him that I wanted him to follow his own wishes. Shortly afterward he announced for the second term. . . .

Sometimes I am asked whether I enjoyed being First Lady. In a way, yes. I rejoiced that I could help Ike perform another big task, for which I think he was predestined. On the other hand, I never sought or wanted any prominence in my own right.

Running the White House, I might add, is a big and time-consuming responsibility. Despite the fact that a First Lady has a lot of skilled help around the place, the job still requires much supervision from the top if things are to run smoothly. I also had a constant struggle with our personal financial budget to make ends meet.

Many people think the government supplies everything for the President, but this certainly

Top: Ike and John Foster Dulles in 1956.
Bottom: The First and Second Families on Election Eve,
November 5, 1956.

isn't true. The government foots the bills for official entertaining, but it doesn't pay for the personal food and other expenses of the President and his family or for political entertaining, of which there is a great deal. I don't profess to know what other "first families" have done, but Ike and I were scrupulous about such matters. We had our own personal budget, and I never used *anything* from government supplies. When my mother came to live with us for a time in the White House, she insisted on helping us by paying for her board and her maid. And Ike paid personally for any entertaining which he regarded as political. In a borderline case, he still took it out of our personal funds.

One of the most enjoyable periods in our entire life was the first five years after we left the White House—before Ike's second heart attack in November 1965, and the gradual decline of his health which followed. Although he still worked hard during his years of so-called retirement—at his writing and in meeting the still great public demands upon him—it was, relatively speaking, a time of relaxation. We had more time to enjoy the pleasant business of just living.

We had completed the building and furnishing of our Gettysburg house while we were still in Washington and so were able to move in the day we left the White House. Ike loved the Gettysburg place, not only the house but the farm —the cattle, the growing things, the pastures and the beautiful woods. Despite a long life far from agriculture, he had an affinity for the soil. He pored over books on farming and cattle and came to know a great deal about these things. He took great satisfaction in the fact that our lands became far more fertile under his ownership. He had what he called our kitchen garden, and he was never prouder than when he could bring in a hamper of fine tomatoes or a basket of beans to show me.

After we left the White House, Ike had more time for his beloved game of golf. Another way he relaxed was to listen to classical music. He spent many long evenings reading or painting, with our stereo playing softly in the background, and when we got a stereo in our car it was a real joy to him. He also liked certain television programs.

John and his lovely wife Barbara and their four children were always a great satisfaction to Ike. Some of his happiest moments were the days when those youngsters came to visit. When John's own book, *The Bitter Woods*, which I believe is now considered the definitive book on the World War II Battle of the Bulge, was published during the final months of Ike's illness, it buoyed him up tremendously. Earlier, when he had read it in manuscript form, he turned to me after he finished the last page and said: "Hell, Mamie, it's *good.*" That was all, but I could see the pride shining in his eyes.

Ike was not a demonstrative man with any of his family—not even with me. Often when he came home from work, his greeting would be merely an affectionate pinch or a pat on the back. It was enough. He didn't have to tell me a dozen times a day how he felt about me.

On Christmas morning of 1968, he handed me a beautiful letter which he had written to me the day before, propped up there in his hospital bed. Among other things, he said that in gratitude he had given a few Christmas remembrances to his nurses and members of the hospital staff who had helped keep him on this earth long enough to wish me "one more Merry Christmas."

When I read those words, I realized that Ike knew this was our last Christmas together. Later I shed a few tears and put that lovely, brave letter away among my most treasured possessions.

Ike in January of 1961, just before he left the White House.

'White Hats and Black'

As a boy, the future President could be rebellious about schoolwork, but he rebelled not at all at reading heavy works of ancient history. There, and in books about George Washington, Dwight Eisenhower found the heroes after whom he would pattern his life:

... The battles of Marathon, Zama, Salamis, and Cannae became as familiar to me as the games (and battles) I enjoyed with my brothers and friends in the school yard. In later years, the movies taught children that the bad guy was the one in the black hat. Such people as Hannibal, Caesar, Pericles, Socrates, Themistocles, Miltiades, and Leonidas were my white hats, my heroes. . . .

When I got around to the Americans, Washington was my hero. I never tired of reading about his exploits at Princeton, at Trenton, and particularly in Valley Forge. . . . The qualities that excited my admiration were Washington's stamina and patience in adversity, first, and then his indomitable courage, daring, and capacity for self-sacrifice.

The beauty of his character always impressed me. While the cherry tree story may be pure legend, his Farewell Address, his counsels to his countrymen, on the occasions such as his speech at Newburgh to the rebellious officers of his Army, exemplified the human qualities I frankly idolized.

'A Strong Family' *Yet stronger than his love of heroes was young Dwight's love and respect for his family. He would remember that family in these words, written near the end of his life:*

Mother and Father maintained a genuine partnership in raising their six sons. Father was the breadwinner, Supreme Court, and Lord High Executioner. Mother was tutor and manager of our household. Their partnership was ideal. This may sound unbelievable, and only recollected in tranquility, but I never heard a cross word pass between them. Never did I hear them disagree on a value judgment in family, social, or economic affairs—not that there weren't sufficient causes. I never had any indication that they were annoyed with each other. Before their children, they were not demonstrative in their love for each other, but a quiet, mutual devotion permeated our home. This had its lasting effect on all the boys.

I may exhibit a son's prejudice. But my feeling reflects the affection and respect of all who knew [my mother]. Her serenity, her open smile, her gentleness with all and her tolerance of their ways, despite an inflexible loyalty to her religious convictions and her own strict pattern of personal conduct, made even a brief visit with Ida Eisenhower memorable for a stranger. And for her sons, privileged to spend a boyhood in her company, the memories are indelible.

[The] willingness of [my] brothers to aid each other was one consequence of the guidance we received as youngsters. Years later, when Arthur was an authority on grain marketing, finance and banking, Edgar a successful lawyer and director of industrial companies, Earl a radio station owner and public relations director of the community newspaper, Milton president of Johns Hopkins University, and I a first administration Republican President, friends often asked why there had not been a black sheep in the family.

I have often thought about this. The answer

The parents to whom Ike was so devoted--
David Jacob and Ida Eisenhower on their
50th wedding anniversary.

lies, I think, in the fact that our family life was free from parental quarreling and filled with genuine, if not demonstrated love. I never knew anyone from a divorced family until I went to West Point. Responsibility was a part of maturing. Concern for others was natural in our small community. And ambition without arrogance was quietly instilled in us by both parents. Part of that ambition was self-dependence.

All in all, we were a cheerful and a vital family. Our pleasures were simple—they included survival—but we had plenty of fresh air, exercise, and companionship. We would have been insulted had anyone offered us charity; instead my mother was always ready to take some of her home remedies or food and start out to help anyone who was sick or suffering. The daily prayers of my parents did not fail to include a plea for the hungry, the weary, and the unfortunates of the world.

"Responsible Citizenship" in a free country means what it says. It means conducting one's self responsibly, in the interest of others as well as self.   D.D.E.

'Mr. Eisenhower's Solution'

At West Point, Cadet Eisenhower continued to rebel from schoolwork, but his exceptional intelligence came to his aid. One day in calculus class he was caught unprepared. To his own surprise he came up with a new solution to the problem:

After trying several solutions that seemed to relate, at least remotely, to the one I dimly remembered from the morning before, I encountered nothing but failure. Finally, with only minutes remaining, I worked out one approach that looked fairly reasonable. No one could have been more amazed than I when this line of action agreed exactly with the answer already written on the board. I carefully went over the work, sat down, and awaited my turn to recite. I was the last man in the section to be called upon.

With some trepidation I started in. It took me a short time to explain my simple solution—indeed it had to be simple or I never would have stumbled upon it. At the end, the instructor turned on me angrily and said, "Mr. Eisenhower, it is obvious that you know nothing whatsoever about this problem. You memorized the answer, put down a lot of figures and steps that have no meaning whatsoever, and then wrote out the answer in the hope of fooling the instructor."

I hadn't been well prepared but this was tantamount to calling me a cheat, something that no cadet could be expected to take calmly. I reacted heatedly and started to protest. Just then I heard Major Bell, the Associate Professor of Mathematics (whom we called "Poopy," a name that was always applied to anyone at West Point who was above average in academic attainments) who had entered the room for one of his occasional inspections, interrupting. "Just a minute, Captain."

Of course, I recognized the voice of authority and shut up, although according to my classmates' description that night I was not only red-necked and angry but ready to fight the entire academic department. I would have been kicked out on a charge of insubordination if I had not been stopped.

Major Bell spoke to the instructor, "Captain, please have Mr. Eisenhower go through that solution again."

I did so but in such an emotional state that it is a wonder that I could track it through. The long search for a solution and its eventual simplicity stood me in good stead.

Major Bell heard it out and then said, "Captain, Mr. Eisenhower's solution is more logical and easier than the one we've been using. I'm surprised that none of us, supposedly good mathematicians, has stumbled on it. It will be incorporated in our procedures from now on."

This was a blessing. A moment before, I had an excellent chance of being expelled in disgrace from the Academy. Now, at least with one officer, I was sitting on top of the world.

'I Was Intrigued' *After West Point, from which he graduated in 1915, Cadet Eisenhower was commissioned a second lieutenant in the infantry and began training men for war. Mrs. Eisenhower offered her version of her meeting with Dwight Eisenhower in the introduction to this book. Here is her husband's version, from his reminiscence* At Ease:

One Sunday afternoon in October, as Officer of the Day, I walked out of the Bachelor Officers Quarters to make an inspection of guard posts. On the walk across the street was a small group of people, one of whom was Lulu Harris, the

wife of Major Hunter Harris and a lady popular with all the second lieutenants of the post.

"Ike," she called, "won't you come over here? I have some people I'd like you to meet."

"Sorry, Mrs. Harris," I called back, "I'm on guard and have to start an inspection trip."

She then turned to one young girl, as I discovered later, and said, "Humph! The woman-hater of the post."

Naturally, this caught the attention of the girl, who said something to Mrs. Harris that caused her to call once more. "We didn't ask you to come over to *stay*. Just come over here and meet these friends of mine."

I hadn't any objection and so, in guard uniform, which was olive drab with campaign hat and blouse and sidearms, I walked stiffly across the street to say a polite greeting to the little family gathered around Mrs. Harris. Their name was Doud. They were from Denver and they spent the winter months each year in San Antonio. Out for a ride in a large car, they had stopped to pay a brief call on their friend, Lulu Harris. The one who attracted my eye instantly was a vivacious and attractive girl, smaller than average, saucy in the look about her face and in her whole attitude. If she had been intrigued by my reputation as a woman-hater, I was intrigued by her appearance. I said that I had to make the rounds of all the guard posts and asked whether she would like to go along.

To my astonishment, she turned to her mother, said a few words, and went off with me. Eventually I found out that one of the things that she was least fond of—to put it mildly— was walking. But apparently the little colloquy that had taken place, especially Lulu Harris' remark, caused her to take a second look at the Second Lieutenant who seemed rather brash or indifferent. Possibly she went along just to take me down a peg. In any event, that was the entrance into my life of Mamie Geneva Doud.

'The Greatest Disappointment'

The chance meeting led to courtship and then to marriage. By 1920, the Eisenhowers were living at Camp Meade with their young son Icky. It was a happy life until tragedy struck:

Mamie, Icky, and I had settled down to a fuller family life than we'd ever known. Icky, naturally, was in his element, and he thoroughly enjoyed his role as the center of attention. For a little boy just getting interested in the outside world, few places could have been more exciting than Meade. Deafening noises of the tanks enthralled him. A football scrimmage was pure delight. And a parade with martial music set him aglow. I was inclined to display Icky and his talents at the slightest excuse, or without one, for that matter. In his company, I'm sure I strutted a bit and Mamie was thoroughly happy that, once again, her two men were with her.

By now, I was entirely out of debt. Perhaps we were in a position to enjoy an amenity or two. Possibly we could afford a maid who would help Mamie in a makeshift house that required constant attention. We hired a girl in the neighborhood who was ready to work and who seemed both pleasant and efficient. When she accepted the job, the chain of circumstances began, linking us to a tragedy from which we never recovered.

We learned later that just before we met her the girl had suffered an attack of scarlet fever. Although her cure was quick and she showed no evidence of illness, the doctors finally concluded that she had brought the disease to the camp—and that our young son had contracted it from her.

We did everything possible to save him. The camp doctor brought in specialists from the nearby Johns Hopkins Medical School in Baltimore. During his illness, the doctor did not allow me into his room. But there was a porch on which I was allowed to sit and I could look into the room and wave to him. Occasionally, they would let me come to the door just to speak to Icky. I haunted the halls of the hospital. Hour after hour, Mamie and I could only hope and pray. In those days, before modern medicine eliminated scarlet fever as a childhood scourge, hope and prayer were the only possibilities for parents. At the turn of the year, we lost our first-born son.

This was the greatest disappointment and disaster in my life, the one I have never been able to forget completely. Today when I think of it, even now as I write of it, the keenness of our loss comes back to me as fresh and as terrible as it was in that long dark day soon after Christmas, 1920. . . .

In the months that followed, no matter what activities and preoccupations there were, we could never forget the death of the boy.

'Tempers Are Short!'

Dwight Eisenhower reported to the War Department from the Philippines on December 14, 1941, one week after Pearl Harbor. His first task was to devise a plan of action for strengthening the Western Pacific, where the situation was critical. He planned to use Australia for a Pacific base of operations. Delays and confusion angered him, and on January 4, 1942, he wrote himself this note:

Tempers are short! There are lots of amateur strategists on the job—and prima donnas everywhere. I'd give anything to be back in the field. It's hard to get anything done in Australia. Dive bombers arrived minus essential parts—base facilities are meager. Other expeditions, directed by politicians, interfere, notably, Magnet and Gymnast. But we are getting some things on the way to Australia. The air plan is four pursuit, two heavy bomber, two medium bomber, one light bombardment groups. We are trying to ship staff and personnel needed. But we have got to have ships!! And we need them now.

'You May Be the Man'

General George Marshall asked Eisenhower to prepare a directive to the Commanding General, U.S. Forces, British Isles. On June 8, 1942, Eisenhower delivered the document to Marshall. It provided for "unified command of all American forces allocated to the European area." Eisenhower recalls the moment in Crusade in Europe:

I remarked to General Marshall that this was one paper he should read in detail before it went out because it was likely to be an important document in the further waging of the war. His reply still lives in my memory: "I certainly do want to read it. You may be the man who executes it. If that's the case, when can you leave?" Three days later General Marshall told me definitely that I would command the European theater.

'Inconsequential Thoughts'

Supreme Commander Eisenhower soon realized that the American plan to strike first at Europe could not be put into execution until a massive buildup of troops and material had been accomplished. The Allies decided instead to invade Africa and then Italy, and Eisenhower moved his command from London to Gibraltar. Waiting for invasion reports, the Supreme Commander wrote this note to himself on November 9, 1942:

Inconsequential thoughts of a commander during one of the interminable "waiting periods."

War brings about strange, sometimes ridiculous situations. In my service I've often thought or dreamed of commands of various types that I might one day hold—war commands, peace commands, battle commands, administrative commands, etc. One I now have could never, under any conditions, have entered my mind even fleetingly. *I have operational command of Gibraltar!!* The symbol of the solidity of the British Empire—the hallmark of safety and security at home—the jealously guarded rock that has played a tremendous part in the trade development of the English race! An American is in charge and I am he. Hundreds of feet within the bowels of the Rock itself I have my CP (Command Post). I simply *must* have a grandchild or I'll never have the fun of telling this when I'm fishing, grey-bearded, on the banks of a quiet bayou in the deep south.

Again—what soldier ever took the trouble to contemplate the possibility of holding an *Allied* Command. And of all things, an Allied Command of ground, air and naval forces? Usually we pity the soldier of history that had to work with Allies. But we don't now, and through months of work we've rather successfully integrated the forces and the commands and staffs of British and American contingents—now we have to get together with the North African French! Just how the French angle will develop only the future can tell, but I am proud of this British-U.S. command! The final result I don't know—but I do know that every element of my command—all U.S. and British services are working together beautifully and harmoniously! That's something. . . .

'The Great Crusade'

General Eisenhower's determination that operation OVERLORD (the invasion of France) would bring a quick end to the war is obvious in this message to the troops of the Allied Expeditionary Forces on June 6, 1944, the morning of the invasion:

Soldiers, Sailors and Airmen of the Allied Expeditionary Forces: You are about to embark upon the Great Crusade, toward which we have striven these many months. The eyes of the world are upon you. The hopes and prayers of liberty-loving people everywhere march with you. In company with our brave Allies and brothers-in-arms on other Fronts you will bring about the destruction of the German war machine, the elimination of Nazi tyranny over oppressed peoples of Europe, and security for ourselves in a free world.

Your task will not be an easy one. Your enemy is well trained, well equipped and battle-hardened. He will fight savagely.

But this is the year 1944! Much has happened since the Nazi triumphs of 1940-41. The United Nations have inflicted upon the Germans great defeats, in open battle, man-to-man. Our air

offensive has seriously reduced their strength in the air and their capacity to wage war on the ground. Our Home Fronts have given us an overwhelming superiority in weapons and munitions of war, and placed at our disposal great reserves of trained fighting men. The tide has turned! The free men of the world are marching together to Victory!

I have full confidence in your courage, devotion to duty and skill in battle. We will accept nothing less than full victory!

Good Luck! And let us all beseech the blessing of Almighty God upon this great and noble undertaking.

Never negotiate with an adversary except from a position of strength.   D.D.E.

General Dwight D. Eisenhower, Supreme Allied Commander, inspects an Infantry unit in England.

'I Guess It's Not So Bad'

The fighting in France continued through the summer of 1944. By March 1945, General Eisenhower and his troops had reached the banks of the Rhine. And even there, facing Germany on the eve of one of the final assaults of the war, the General found time to concern himself not only with the total strategy but with his individual men:

Because the batteries were distributed on the flat plains on the western bank of the Rhine every flash could be seen. The din was incessant. Meanwhile infantry assault troops were marching up to the water's edge to get into the boats. We joined some of them and found the troops remarkably eager to finish the job. There is no substitute for a succession of great victories in building morale. Nevertheless, as we walked along I fell in with one young soldier who seemed silent and depressed.

"How are you feeling, son?" I asked.

"General," he said, "I'm awful nervous. I was wounded two months ago and just got back from the hospital yesterday. I don't feel so good!"

"Well," I said to him, "you and I are a good

pair then, because I'm nervous too. But we've planned this attack for a long time and we've got all the planes, the guns, and airborne troops we can use to smash the Germans. Maybe if we just walk along together to the river we'll be good for each other."

"Oh," he said, "I meant I *was* nervous; I'm not any more. I guess it's not so bad around here." And I knew what he meant.

'The Rejoicing Bells Peal Forth'

At last the war was won. The Supreme Commander found himself of more than two minds about it. One expression of his attitude came on May 8, 1945, in his V-E Day radio speech broadcast to the United States —his belief that the war had been a crusade for human freedom:

So—history's mightiest machine of conquest has been utterly destroyed. The deliberate design of brutal, world-wide rape that the German nation eagerly absorbed from the diseased brain of Hitler, has met the fate decreed for it by outraged justice. The self-styled super-race that six years ago set out on a career of pillage is now groveling amongst the ruins of its own shattered cities as it fearfully hopes for a better fate than it inflicted upon its own helpless victims. Throughout the United Nations the rejoicing bells peal forth.

Those bells voice our happiness that the Nazi scourge has been eliminated from the earth. But for the remaining enemy of humankind—Japan —those bells are sounding an imminent doom. The complete armed might of liberty and freedom is at last free to turn from the elimination of the principal criminal to the punishment of its equally despicable satellite. Already our comrades in the Pacific have made great inroads into her vitals. Japan herself must now realize her fate is sealed.

All of us here have one underlying ambition; to return speedily to our families. But we entered this war to do our duty to our country and to the cause that remains as sacred today as on that December 7th when we suddenly found ourselves at war. Wherever any man is called he will continue to do his part in assuring the completeness of victory. Some of us will stay here to police the areas and the nation that we have conquered, so that systems of justice and of order may prevail. Some will be called upon to participate in the Pacific war. But some—and I trust in ever-increasing numbers—will soon experience the joy of returning home.

I speak for the more than three million Americans in this Theater in saying that, when we are so fortunate as to come back to you, there need be no welcoming parades, no special celebrations. All we ask is to come back into the warmth of the hearts we left behind and to resume once more pursuits of peace—under our own American conceptions of liberty and of right, in which our beloved country has always dwelt.

We look upon this shaken earth, and we declare our firm and fixed purpose—the building of peace with justice in a world where moral law prevails.   D. D. E.

The Guildhall Address

General Eisenhower developed another point of view about the war in his justly celebrated Guildhall Address, delivered in London on June 12, 1945, after London presented him with honorary citizenship. Before the leaders and the peoples of Great Britain he affirmed his belief in the bonds that joined the British and the American peoples, the bonds of common faith in democracy. Here are some excerpts from that momentous speech:

The only attitude in which a commander may with satisfaction receive the tributes of his friends is in the humble acknowledgment that no matter how unworthy he may be, his position is the symbol of great human forces that have labored arduously and successfully for a righteous cause. Unless he feels this symbolism and this rightness in what he has tried to do, then he is disregardful of courage, fortitude, and devotion of the vast multitudes he has been honored to command. If all Allied men and women that have served with me in this war can only know that it is they whom this august body is really honoring today, then indeed I will be content.

A triumphant Eisenhower delivers the famous Guildhall Address in London.

I am not a native of this land. I come from the very heart of America. In the superficial aspects by which we ordinarily recognize family relationships, the town where I was born and the one where I was reared are far separated from this great city. Abilene, Kansas, and Denison, Texas, would together equal in size, possibly one five-hundredth of a part of great London.

Yet kinship among nations is not determined in such measurements as proximity, size, and age. Rather we should turn to those inner things— call them what you will—I mean those intangibles that are the real treasures free men possess.

To preserve his freedom of worship, his equality before law, his liberty to speak and act as he sees fit, subject only to provisions that he trespass not upon similar rights of others—a Londoner will fight. So will a citizen of Abilene.

When we consider these things, then the valley of the Thames draws closer to the farms of Kansas and the plains of Texas.

To my mind it is clear that when two peoples will face the tragedies of war to defend the same spiritual values, the same treasured rights, then in the deepest sense those two are truly related. So even as I proclaim my undying Americanism, I am bold enough and exceedingly proud to claim the basis of kinship to you of London.

My most cherished hope is that after Japan joins the Nazis in utter defeat, neither my country nor yours need ever again summon its sons and daughters from their peaceful pursuits to face the tragedies of battle. But—a fact important for both of us to remember—neither London nor Abilene, sisters under the skin, will sell her birthright for physical safety, her liberty for mere existence.

No petty differences in the world of trade, traditions, or national pride should ever blind us to our identities in priceless values.

If we keep our eyes on this guidepost, then no difficulties along our path of mutual co-operation can ever be insurmountable. Moreover, when this truth has permeated to the remotest hamlet and heart of all peoples, then indeed may we beat our swords into plowshares and all nations can enjoy the fruitfulness of the earth.

'The Tragedy...
Was Immense'

Still another view informs this profound statement about war from General Eisenhower's book At Ease:

War, as so many men have said, is the most stupid and tragic of human ventures. It is stupid because so few problems are enduringly solved; tragic because its cost in lives and spirit and treasure is seldom matched in the fruits of victory. Still, I never intend to join myself with those who damn all wars as vile crimes against humanity. World War II, not sought by the people of the United States or its allies, was certainly not, on their part, either stupid or in vain. Satisfaction, and memories beyond price, rewarded those who survived and who, in loyalty to country and ideals, answered the attacks.

The tragedy of it all was immense. From the Sunday morning when unarmed church parties of our men died under hundreds of Japanese bombs . . . to the final days when men, women, and children of Japan perished under two bombs at Hiroshima and Nagasaki, millions died. The loss of lives that might have been creatively lived scars the mind of the modern world.

'A Middle Way' On January 20,

1953, Dwight David Eisenhower became the 34th President of the United States. A month after his inauguration, in his State of the Union message to Congress, President Eisenhower articulated the dominant method of his Presidency, his search for a "middle way":

As our heart summons our strength, our wisdom must direct it.

There is, in world affairs, a steady course to be followed between an assertion of strength that is truculent and a confession of helplessness that is cowardly.

There is, in our affairs at home, a middle way between untrammeled freedom of the individual and the demands for the welfare of the whole nation. This way must avoid government by bureaucracy as carefully as it avoids neglect of the helpless.

In every area of political action, free men must think before they can expect to win.

In this spirit we must live and labor: confident of our strength, compassionate in our heart, clear in our mind.

In this spirit, let us together turn to the great tasks before us.

'A Cross of Iron'

Seeking, as his speech writers tell us in their memoirs, some concrete way to dramatize the futility of the Cold War, President Eisenhower hit upon the idea of comparing peaceful expenditures with the expenditures both the United States and the Soviet Union were making for armaments. Then he capped the comparison with a brilliant allusion to William Jennings Bryan's famous phrase "a cross of gold":

Every gun made, every warship launched, every rocket fired signifies, in the final sense, a theft from those who hunger and are not fed, those who are cold and not clothed.

This world in arms is not spending money alone.

It is spending the sweat of its laborers, the genius of its scientists, the hopes of its children.

The cost of one modern heavy bomber is this: a modern brick school in more than thirty cities.

It is two electric power plants, each serving a town of 60,000 population.

It is two fine, fully equipped hospitals.

It is some fifty miles of concrete highway.

We pay for a single fighter plane with a half

million bushels of wheat.

We pay for a single destroyer with new homes that could have housed more than 80,000 people.

This, I repeat, is the best way of life to be found on the road the world has been taking.

This is not a way of life at all, in any true sense. Under the cloud of threatening war, it is humanity hanging from a cross of iron.

We are persuaded by necessity and by belief that the strength of all free peoples lies in unity; their danger, in discord.   D.D.E.

'Don't Join the Book Burners'

President Eisenhower was roundly condemned for refusing to attack Joseph McCarthy for his irresponsible witch-hunting. The President knew better, however: knew that if he attacked McCarthy, the conservative Republicans who had preferred Taft to Eisenhower in the first place would rally round their Senate colleague. But the President did not remain silent. At Dartmouth College he exhorted the students to find a better way:

Don't join the book burners. Don't think you are going to conceal faults by concealing evidence that they never existed. Don't be afraid to go in your library and read every book, as long as that document does not offend our own ideas of decency. That should be the only censorship.

How will we defeat communism unless we know what it is, and what it teaches, and why does it have such an appeal for men, why are so many people swearing allegiance to it? It is almost a religion, albeit one of the nether regions.

And we have got to fight it with something better, not try to conceal the thinking of our own people. They are part of America. And even if they think ideas that are contrary to

ours, their right to say them, their right to re-
cord them, and their right to have them at
places where they are accessible to others is un-
questioned, or it isn't America.

'A Simple Prayer for Peace'

*It must have seemed para-
doxical to some that one of the world's great
military leaders should be so single-mindedly
dedicated to peace as was President Eisenhower.
It was the major concern of his Presidency, a
concern he certainly learned from his peace-lov-
ing mother, Ida Stover Eisenhower. Here he
speaks of peace on the occasion of the lighting
of the National Community Christmas Tree in
Washington in 1955:*

Peace is the right of every human being. It is
hungered for by all of the peoples of the earth.
So we can be sure that tonight in the fullness of
our hearts and in the spirit of the season, that as
we utter a simple prayer for peace we will be
joined by the multitudes of the earth.

Those multitudes will include rulers as well
as the humblest citizen of lands; the great and

the meek; the proud and the poor; the successful and the failures; the dispirited and the hope-
fuls.

Now each of those prayers will of course dif-
fer according to the characteristics and the per-
sonality of the individual uttering it, but running through every single one of those prayers
will be a thought something of this kind:

May each of us strive to do our best to bring
about better understanding in the world. And
may the infinite peace from above live with us
and be ours forever, and may we live in the confident hope that it will come.

Whatever America hopes to bring to pass
in the world, must first come to pass in
the heart of America.   D.D.E.

Top: Ike and his favorite hobby. He was quite an
accomplished painter.
Bottom: Ike and Mamie celebrate Christmas 1955,
with son John and family.

'To Promote Human Happiness'

In December 1959, President Eisenhower's search for peace became a personal quest and he embarked on an eleven-nation goodwill tour. His purpose was to acquaint the world with American ideals. He left this country with some inspiring parting remarks:

In every country I hope to make widely known America's deepest desire—a world in which all nations may prosper in freedom, justice, and peace, unmolested and unafraid.

I shall try to convey to everyone our earnestness in striving to reduce the tensions dividing mankind—an effort first requiring, as indeed Mr. Khrushchev agrees, the beginning of mutual disarmament. Of course, I shall stress that the first requirement for mutual disarmament is mutual verification.

Then I hope to make this truth clear—that, on all this earth, not anywhere does our Nation seek territory, selfish gain or unfair advantage for itself. I hope all can understand that beyond her shores, as at home, America aspires only to promote human happiness, justly achieved.

Our country has been unjustly described as one pursuing only materialistic goals; as building a culture whose hallmarks are gadgets and shallow pleasures; as prizing wealth above ideals, machines above spirit, leisure above learning, and war above peace.

Actually, as our declaration proclaims, the core of our Nation is belief in a Creator who has endowed all men with inalienable rights, including life, liberty, and the pursuit of happiness. In that belief is our country's true hallmark—a faith that permeates every aspect of our political, social, and family life. This truth, too, I hope to emphasize abroad.

One last thought. We have heard much of the phrase, "Peace and friendship." This phrase, in expressing the aspirations of America, is not complete. We should say instead, "Peace and friendship, in freedom." This, I think, is America's real message to the world.

The U-2 Incident

For President Eisenhower, the U-2 incident of early May 1960, was a personal blow. He had placed great hope in his goodwill tours. The entire free world had hoped with him that his efforts would result in peacemaking with the Soviet Union. But the President found no cause for despair, only anger that the Soviet obsession with secrecy should make so much of so little. His reply contained four main points:

The first point is this: the need for intelligence-gathering activities.

No one wants another Pearl Harbor. This means that we must have knowledge of military forces and preparations around the world, especially those capable of massive surprise attacks.

Secrecy in the Soviet Union makes this essential. In most of the world no large-scale attack could be prepared in secret, but in the Soviet Union there is a fetish of secrecy and conceal-ment. This is a major cause of international tension and uneasiness today. Our deterrent must never be placed in jeopardy. The safety of the whole free world demands this.

President Eisenhower fields a question during a news conference.

My second point: the nature of intelligence-gathering activities.

These have a special and secret character. They are, so to speak, "below the surface" activities.

We do not use our Army, Navy, or Air Force for this purpose, first, to avoid any possibility of the use of force in connection with these activities, and second, because our military forces, for obvious reasons, cannot be given latitude under broad directives but must be kept under strict control in every detail.

These activities have their own rules and methods of concealment which seek to mislead and obscure—just as in the Soviet allegations there are many discrepancies. For example, there is some reason to believe that the plane in question was not shot down at high altitude. The normal agencies of our government are unaware of these specific activities or of the special efforts to conceal them.

Third point: how should we view all of this activity?

It is a distasteful but vital necessity.

We prefer and work for a different kind of world—and a different way of obtaining the information essential to confidence and effective deterrents. Open societies, in the day of present weapons, are the only answer.

My final point is that we must not be distracted from the real issues of the day by what is an incident or a symptom of the world situation today.

This incident has been given great propaganda exploitation. The emphasis given to a flight of an unarmed nonmilitary plane can only reflect a fetish of secrecy.

The real issues are the ones we will be working on at the summit—disarmament, search for solutions affecting Germany and Berlin, and the whole range of East-West relations, including the reduction of secrecy and suspicion.

Frankly, I am hopeful that we may make progress on these great issues. This is what we mean when we speak of "working for peace."

A sound peace—with security, justice, well-being, and freedom for the people of the world *can* be achieved, but only by patiently and thoughtfully following a hard and sure and tested road.   D.D.E.

'A Matter of Brief Incidents'

Retired from the Presidency, General Eisenhower found time to reflect candidly on his many years of leadership and public service. His remarks, in his extraordinary book At Ease: Stories I Tell To Friends, *are savorings of the deepest philosophy:*

Earlier, I said that I had been struck with the notion that time flies. But now, that second idea persists in my mind—that the making of history, the shaping of human lives, is more a matter of brief incidents, quiet talks, chance encounters, sudden flashes of leadership or inspiration, and sometimes simple routine than it is of heroes, headlines, grand pronouncements, or widely heralded decisions.

Great concepts, great ideals, great decisions, can be the engines which move men to greatness themselves. But the documents which express them are sometimes sterile things unless there are people to cause inspiration to flow from them. My good fortune has been a lifetime of continuous association with men and women, widely different, who sometimes in a few minutes by word of mouth, or sometimes over

Ike and Mamie at their Gettysburg farm in 1956.

the years by their example, gave others inspiration and guidance. They gave me encouragement or helped me to prepare.

Set at The Castle Press in Trump Medieval,
a Venetian typeface designed by
Professor Georg Trump, Munich.
Printed on Hallmark Eggshell Book paper.
Designed by Claudia Becker.

President Eisenhower holds a White House
conference with John Foster Dulles, Winston Churchill,
and Anthony Eden.